Autumn Dream's
A Fall Vision Board Clip Art Book

Forward to Fall

Welcome to a journey where the essence of Fall is your companion, guiding your dreams to new heights! If you are ready for a season of transformation and manifestation, you've chosen the right book!

This book is a curated collection of over 660+ images and elements designed to align your thoughts, emotions, and actions with the positive energies of Autumn.

It's here to help you channel your focus and energize your manifestations with the serene energy of the season, influencing your day-to-day life and imbuing it with positive vibes.

Vision Boards are central to this transformative journey; acting as the canvas upon which our dreams and aspirations are painted. Through the power of visualization, you will be able to bring wonderful and amazing things into your life!

What is Visualization?

Visualization is a practical mind exercise involving the formation of mental images representing your goals, moods, or desired outcomes. It is a cornerstone in self-improvement and goal attainment, while also serving to enhance mood and induce relaxation.

The Visualization Technique is a beacon; guiding you towards your dreams by sharpening your focus, improving your motivation, bolstering your confidence, and turning your aspirations into your reality.

What are Vision Boards?

Vision Boards are practical and effective visualization tools. They are physical representations of your dreams, aspirations or overall mood influencers created by assembling photos and words on a board. Vision Boards serve as daily reminders of your goals and desires, helping maintain focus and motivation.

Vision Boards are the tangible counterparts of visualization. They are a collage of your desires and goals, represented through pictures and words collected from diverse sources and assembled on a board. These boards are daily reminders, motivational tools whispering the echoes of your dreams and keeping your gaze fixed on your goals.

Creating Your Vision Board

Creating a vision board is like painting your aspirations on a canvas, and this book is a palette of new elements; offering seasonal colors and creative inspirations to sprinkle on your vision boards - both existing or new - and allowing you to craft masterpieces of inspiration that resonate with your soul.

Fall is a season of transitions, when the blazing rush of summertime fades into a time for reflection and anticipation for the coming months. It is about reaping the rewards and planting seeds for our future abundance. During this season, the manifestation energy is especially potent, with events like the Autumnal Equinox, Harvest Moon, and Hunter's Moon serving as catalysts for our dreams.

As we transition to this period in the year, we can update our vision boards for the things we are anticipating to come, or would like to see in our coming future.

Our Hopes For You

In creating this book, we hope to have curated a collection of images and art where everyone can find something they love and feel inspired by.

We've included elements of varying sizes to ensure versatility in your creations, and aimed to create a diverse and inclusive collection to inspire every reader's creative energy. In addition to Vision Boards, these images also work great for scrapbooking and collage art!

Remember, this book is made for you! Feel free to reshape it; take out pages, clip them to your heart's content, or simply keep it intact for your daily viewing for years to come. Whatever brings you joy and aligns with your aspirations is exactly how it should be used.

So, embrace this journey, let every page be a step towards realizing your dreams, and remember, the autumn leaves are whispering the songs of your future successes!

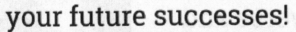

Change is Beautiful

I embrace the beauty of change, just as nature does every fall.

With every leaf that falls I welcome change and growth

Letting Go to Grow

Reflection

Tranquility

The calming whisper of falling leaves is nature's prescription for a relaxed mind.

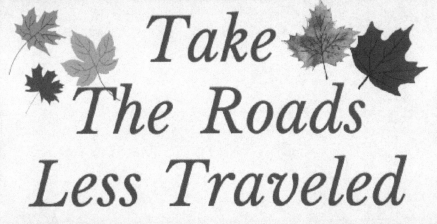

Take
The Roads
Less Traveled

Gather moments.
Not things.

Explore

WANDERLUST

DISCOVERY

Harvest Time

Enjoy the Fruit of Your Labor.

AUTUMN'S HARVEST MIRRORS
THE ABUNDANCE I INVITE
INTO MY LIFE.

SAVORING AUTUMN FLAVORS

SAVORING AUTUMN FLAVORS

NOURISH

Pumpkin Spice

&

Everything Nice

AUTUMN

Lifestyle

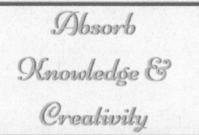

Absorb Knowledge & Creativity

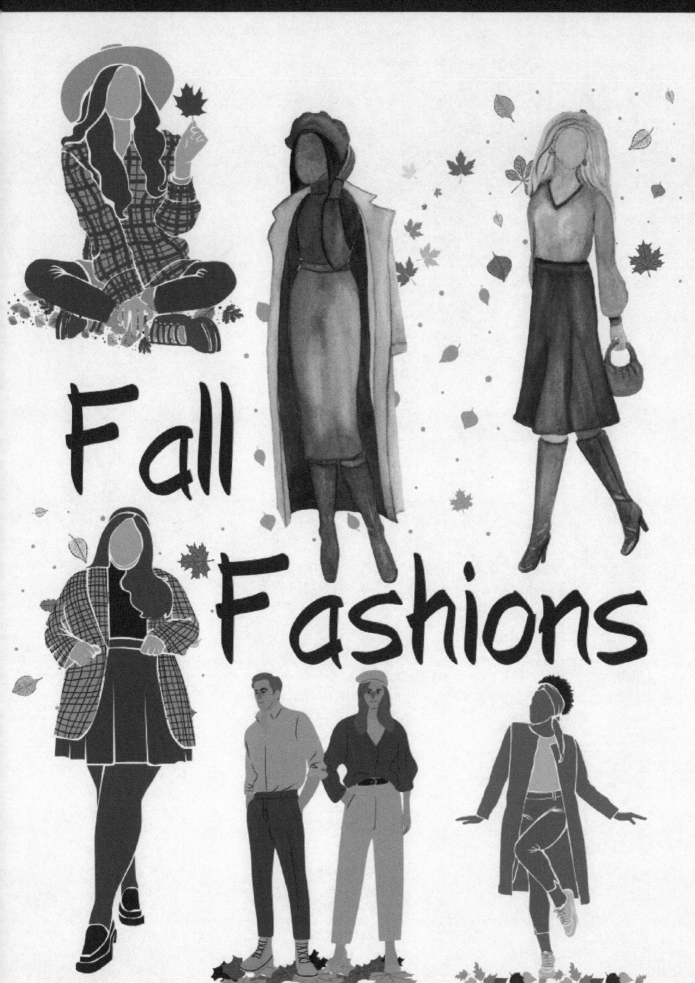

Fall Fashions

Sweater Weather

Vibrance

Radiance

Fall Wedding

Better Together

Together as the leaves Fall

Love as deep as autumn's riches

FRIENDS

&

FAMILY

Furry Friends in Fall

Adopt a Pet

Create &
DECORATE

Treats

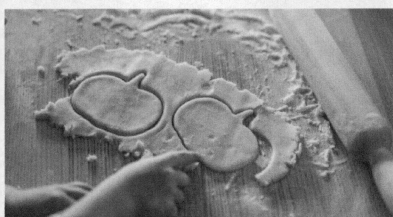

Dream

AUTUMN EQUINOX

Manifest

DAY OF THE DEAD

Giving Thanks

Food

 Fun

Family

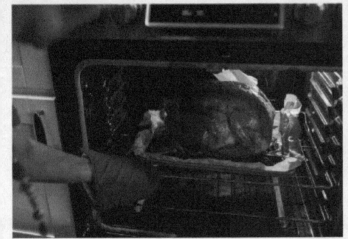

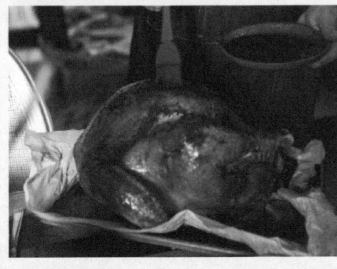

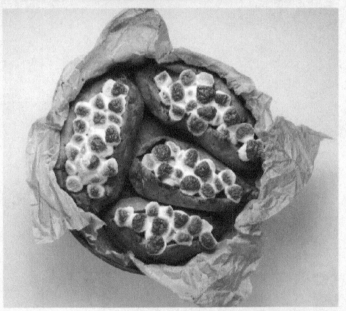

A *Thanksgiving* Prayer

May our home be full of *joy*,
May our *hearts* be knit with love,
As we give our *grateful thanks*
For Thy *blessings* from above.

I Appreciate Everyone Who Sits At My Table

THANKFUL

Words

Quotes

&

Patterns

Add a personal touch to your vision board with these extra elements

Hope

Ask

Goals

Believe

Recieve

Prosper

Improvement

Happy

Intent

GLOW

Heal

Laugh

Home

Live

<u>Sustain</u>

Study

Invest

Gain

Imagine

Give

Intuition

 Travel

Wealth

LOVE

Charity

Health

Survivor

Indulge

 Create

 Heart

Grace

Queen

Complete

Goddess

Past

Present

Warrior

Future

Achieve

Boss

TRANSFORMATION

Today

Now

You Got This 👍

Make It Happen

It's a Great Day

Don't Worry

Everything's Awesome

My Light Shines Bright

I Can Do It

I WILL DO IT

New Day, Fresh Start

Make it Happen

Don't Worry

Everything is Awesome

MAKE IT HAPPEN

I Can Do It

Rustling Leaves
Rustling Ideas

Autumn Adventures
Await

As Seasons Change, So Do I

HARVESTING DREAMS

hello
FALL

*Love and Light, Makes
Everything Right*

Dress in confidence, walk with ambition, and harvest success.

As the world slows with the fall, I take a moment to breathe, relax, and cherish all those around me.

Harvest season is a reminder that my efforts will bear fruit.

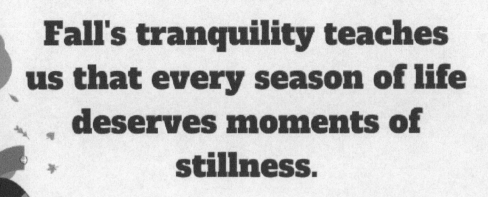

Fall's tranquility teaches us that every season of life deserves moments of stillness.

Success is not just in the harvest, but the seeds you plant in the fall.

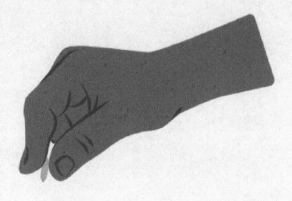

Autumn's richness is a testament to nature's rewards for patience and persistence.

In every falling leaf, there's a lesson about growth, endings, and new beginnings.

Fall's tranquility teaches
us that every season of life
deserves moments of
stillness.

Success is not just
in the harvest, but
the seeds you plant
in the fall

Autumn's richness is a
permanent testament
rewards for patience
and persistence

In every falling leaf,
there's a lesson about
growth, endings, and
new beginnings.